CONTENTS

Milestones and Memories,
A CELEBRATION OF LIFE'S SPECIAL MOMENTS

As avid knitters, we've learned that blankets are really the perfect handmade gift...they don't need to fit the recipient or match a wardrobe, and can easily be enjoyed and cherished for years and years. Pillows are great gifts as well, adding a pop of personality without overwhelming a room's design.

Capture the special moments and celebrate the people in your life with **Milestones & Memories**. Use the modular system of colorwork squares in this book to create an heirloom for your loved ones. Simply choose your size - throw, blanket or pillow - choose your charts, and get knitting! Using basic intarsia and duplicate stitch, the charted designs included are suitable for even knitters new to colorwork.

You can commemorate the wedding day of the dear ones in your life in a way they will both treasure and use, or celebrate that awesome friend with a throw pillow tailor-made to their passions and interests. With over 40 charts to choose from and templates to create your own, you'll be able to find the perfect way to show someone you care with a personalized gift, made with love just for them.

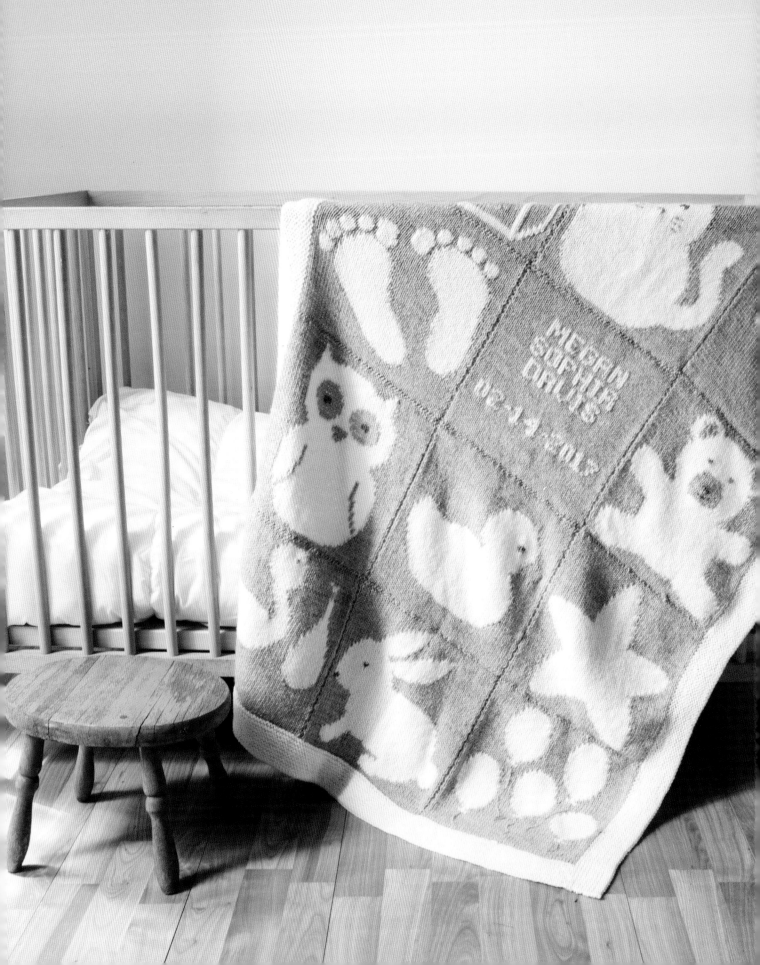

BABY BLANKET

FINISHED MEASUREMENTS
34" x 44"

YARN
Knit Picks Wool of the Andes (100%
Peruvian Highland Wool; 110 yards/50g):
MC Lake Ice Heather 23898, 7 skeins,
C1 White 24065, 7 skeins, C2 Semolina
25064, 1 skein

NEEDLES
US 7 (4.5mm) straight or circular needles,
or size to obtain gauge
US 7 (4.5mm) 40-48" circular needles for
border

NOTIONS
Yarn Needle
Stitch Markers
Scrap yarn in grey and pink

GAUGE
20 sts and 28 rows = 4" in St st, blocked

Baby Blanket

Photographed example features the following charts: Baby Blocks (p.35), Kitty (p. 40), Rattle (p.42), Baby Feet (p. 45), Small Alphabet (p. 65), Teddy Bear (p. 37), Owl (p. 41), Duck (p.38), Star (p. 43). While the chart appears to be rectangular, at gauge they will knit up as a square.

DIRECTIONS

Choose 12 squares from the charts. Each one is knit the same way, adding the colors via intarsia or duplicate stitch. There is a slipped stitch on each end of the square, which will make it easier to seam the squares at the end.

Squares

Loosely CO 52 sts.

Row 1: Sl 1, K row 1 of chart to last st, K1

Row 2: Sl 1, P row 2 of chart to last st, K1

Continue in this manner throughout the square. After completing row 70, BO all stitches loosely.

Rep for all squares. If you prefer a solid square, simply follow the same instructions, omitting the chart.

Finishing

Weave in ends. Block each square to 10" x 10". It is very important to make sure your square blocks to the correct measurements.

Arrange the squares in suggested layout or in 3 squares wide x 4 squares long custom layout. With RS facing and using Mattress st, seam the squares together, using MC or preferred color.

Border

With C1, you will knit a garter st border around the blanket.

Along any side of the afghan, with RS facing PU and knit sts along the edge, being sure to PU 2 sts where squares are joined. Work in garter stitch for 2", BO all sts loosely.

Turn blanket 90 degrees, PU and knit along the edge of the border, PU and knit along blanket edge. Work in garter st for 2". BO all sts loosely.

Turn blanket 90 degrees, PU and knit along the edge of the border, PU and knit along blanket edge. Work in garter st for 2". BO all sts loosely.

Turn blanket 90 degrees, PU and knit along the edge of the border, PU and knit along blanket edge, PU and knit along other edge of border. Work in garter st for 2". BO all sts loosely.

Weave in remaining ends.

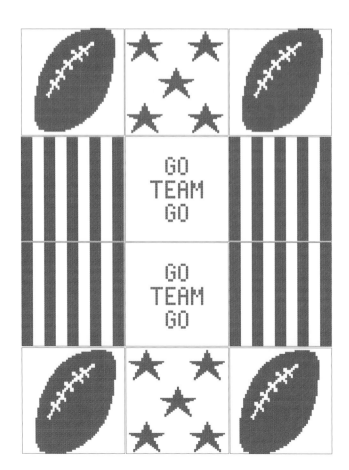

Endless Possibilities

TEAM PLAYER

This book contains 44 charts, featuring mix-and-match designs that celebrate babies & kids, weddings, hobbies, and creative pursuits. Follow the directions for the blanket above to make a sports-themed blanket for the athlete in your life, using the following charts: Football (p. 31), Stars (p. 33), Small Alphabet (p. 65), Vertical Stripes (p. 34).

BABY PILLOW

FINISHED MEASUREMENTS
To fit 20" x 20 pillow form, finished size
21" x 21"

YARN
Knit Picks Wool of the Andes (100%
Peruvian Highland Wool; 110 yards/50g):
MC Clarity 25632, 5 skeins; C1 White
24065; 2 skeins; C2 Wonderland Heather
25068, C3 Crème Brulee 25975, C4
Pumpkin 23430, C5 Pink Posey Heather
25644, C6 Haze Heather 26158, C6 Green
Tea Heather 24648, 1 skein each

NEEDLES
US 7 (4.5mm) straight or circular needles,
or size to obtain gauge
US 7 (4.5mm) 40-48" circular needles for
border

NOTIONS
Yarn Needle
Stitch Markers
20" Pillow Form

GAUGE
20 sts and 28 rows = 4" in St st, blocked

Baby Pillow

Notes: Photographed example features the following charts: Duck (p.38), Owl (p. 41), Bunny (p. 39), Kitty (p. 40). While the chart appears to be rectangular, at gauge they will knit up as a square.

DIRECTIONS
Pillow Front
Choose 4 squares from the charts. Each one is knit the same way, adding the colors via intarsia or duplicate stitch. There is a slipped stitch on each end of the square, which will make it easier to pick up stitches for the border. There are instructions for a plain pillow backing; you can also choose to knit 4 additional squares for decorative back.

Squares
Loosely CO 52 sts.
Row 1: Sl 1, K row 1 of chart to last st, K1
Row 2: Sl 1, P row 2 of chart to last st, K1

Continue in this manner throughout the square. After completing row 70, BO all stitches loosely.

Rep for all squares. If you prefer a solid square, simply follow the same instructions, omitting the chart.

Finishing
Weave in ends. Block each square to 10" x 10".

Arrange the squares in suggested layout or in 2 squares wide x 2 squares long custom layout. With RS facing and using Mattress st, seam the squares together, using MC or preferred color.

Border
With MC, you will knit a small border around the pillow. This will ensure a good fit around your pillow form.

With RS facing and starting with along the right side of the square, *PU 2 (from slipped edge sts), M1 using backward loop CO; rep from * to end of slipped edge sts. Work in St st for 4 rows, BO all sts loosely.

Turn pillow front 90 degrees, PU and K4 along the edge of the border, PU and K along pillow front edge. Work in St st for 4 rows. BO all sts loosely.

Turn pillow front 90 degrees, PU and K4 along the edge of the border, *PU 2 (from slipped edge sts), M1 using backward loop CO; rep from * to end of slipped edge sts. Work in St st for 4 rows, BO all sts loosely

Turn pillow front 90 degrees, PU and K4 along the edge of the border, PU and K along pillow front edge, PU and K4 along edge of border. Work in St st for 4 rows. BO all sts loosely.

Block piece to 21" square.

Pillow Back
With MC, CO 108 sts
Row 1: Sl 1, K across.
Row 2: Sl 1, P to last st, K1

Rep Rows 1-2 for 148 rows or 21".

BO all sts.

Weave in ends and block to 21" square.

With RS facing, seam 3 sides of the pillow using Mattress St. Turn RS out and insert pillow form. Seam remaining side.

Weave in any remaining ends.

Celebrate New Life
WELCOME, BABY!

This book contains 44 charts, featuring mix-and-match designs that celebrate babies & kids, weddings, hobbies, and creative pursuits. Follow the directions for the pillow on page 15 to make a sweet matching gift for the new mom and baby, using the following charts: Baby Bottle (p. 69), Baby Feet (p.45), Teddy Bear (p. 37), Balloons (p. 36).

ADVENTURE PILLOW

FINISHED MEASUREMENTS

To fit 20" x 20 pillow form, finished size
21" x 21"

YARN

Knit Picks Wool of the Andes (100%
Peruvian Highland Wool; 110 yards/50g):
MC Mink Heather 24279, 5 skiens, CC
Shire Heather 25988, 1 skiens

NEEDLES

US 7 (4.5mm) straight or circular needles,
or size to obtain gauge
US 7 (4.5mm) 40-48" circular needles for
border

NOTIONS

Yarn Needle
Stitch Markers
20" Pillow Form

GAUGE

20 sts and 28 rows = 4" in St st, blocked

Adventure Pillow

Notes: Photographed example features the following charts: Boot (p. 55), Bike (p. 54), Camping (p. 56), RV (p. 57). While the charts appears to be rectangular, at gauge they will knit up as a square.

DIRECTIONS
Pillow Front

Choose 4 squares from the charts. Each one is knit the same way, adding the colors via intarsia or duplicate stitch. There is a slipped stitch on each end of the square, which will make it easier to pick up stitches for the border. There are instructions for a plain pillow backing; you can also choose to knit 4 additional squares for decorative back.

Squares

Loosely CO 52 sts.
Row 1: Sl 1, K row 1 of chart to last st, K1
Row 2: Sl 1, P row 2 of chart to last st, K1

Continue in this manner throughout the square. After completing row 70, BO all stitches loosely.

Rep for all squares. If you prefer a solid square, simply follow the same instructions, omitting the chart.

Finishing

Weave in ends. Block each square to 10" x 10".

Arrange the squares in suggested layout or in 2 squares wide x 2 squares long custom layout. With RS facing and using Mattress st, seam the squares together, using MC or preferred color.

Border

With MC, you will knit a small border around the pillow. This will ensure a good fit around your pillow form.

With RS facing and starting with along the right side of the square, *PU 2 (from slipped edge sts), M1 using backward loop CO; rep from * to end of slipped edge sts. Work in St st for 4 rows, BO all sts loosely.

Turn pillow front 90 degrees, PU and K4 along the edge of the border, PU and K along pillow front edge. Work in St st for 4 rows. BO all sts loosely.

Turn pillow front 90 degrees, PU and K4 along the edge of the border, *PU 2 (from slipped edge sts), M1 using backward loop CO; rep from * to end of slipped edge sts. Work in St st for 4 rows, BO all sts loosely

Turn pillow front 90 degrees, PU and K4 along the edge of the border, PU and K along pillow front edge, PU and K4 along edge of border. Work in St st for 4 rows. BO all sts loosely.

Block piece to 21" square.

Pillow Back

CO 108 sts
Row 1: Sl 1, K across.
Row 2: Sl 1, P to last st, K1

Rep Rows 1-2 for 148 rows or 21".

BO all sts.

Weave in ends and block to 21" square.

With RS facing, seam 3 sides of the pillow using Mattress St. Turn RS out and insert pillow form. Seam remaining side.

Weave in any remaining ends.

Limitless Adventure

SHORELINE, AHOY!

This book contains 44 charts, featuring mix-and-match designs that celebrate babies & kids, weddings, hobbies, and creative pursuits. Follow the directions for the pillow above to make a nautical-themed gift for your favorite sailing enthusiast, using the following charts: Anchor (p. 66), Sailboat (p.68), Horizontal Stripes (p. 32).

KITCHEN QUEEN PILLOW

FINISHED MEASUREMENTS

To fit 20" x 20 pillow form, finished size
21" x 21"

YARN

Knit Picks Wool of the Andes (100%
Peruvian Highland Wool; 110 yards/50g):
MC Clarity 25632, 5 skeins; C1 Firecracker
Heather 23896, 2 skeins; C2 Artic Pool
Heather 23894, 2 skeins

NEEDLES

US 7 (4.5mm) straight or circular needles,
or size to obtain gauge
US 7 (4.5mm) 40-48" circular needles for
border

NOTIONS

Yarn Needle
Stitch Markers
20" Pillow Form

GAUGE

20 sts and 28 rows = 4" in St st, blocked

Kitchen Queen Pillow

Notes: Photographed example features the following charts: Mixer (p. 46), Pie (47), Whisk and Spoon (p. 49), Teapot (p. 48). While the charts appears to be rectangular, at gauge they will knit up as a square.

DIRECTIONS
Pillow Front
Choose 4 squares from the charts. Each one is knit the same way, adding the colors via intarsia or duplicate stitch. There is a slipped stitch on each end of the square, which will make it easier to pick up stitches for the border. There are instructions for a plain pillow backing; you can also choose to knit 4 additional squares for decorative back.

Squares
Loosely CO 52 sts.
Row 1: Sl 1, K row 1 of chart to last st, K1
Row 2: Sl 1, P row 2 of chart to last st, K1

Continue in this manner throughout the square. After completing row 70, BO all stitches loosely.

Rep for all squares. If you prefer a solid square, simply follow the same instructions, omitting the chart.

Finishing
Weave in ends. Block each square to 10" x 10".

Arrange the squares in suggested layout or in 2 squares wide x 2 squares long custom layout. With RS facing and using Mattress st, seam the squares together, using MC or preferred color.

Border
With MC, you will knit a small border around the pillow. This will ensure a good fit around your pillow form.

With RS facing and starting with along the right side of the square, *PU 2 (from slipped edge sts), M1 using backward loop CO; rep from * to end of slipped edge sts. Work in St st for 4 rows, BO all sts loosely.

Turn pillow front 90 degrees, PU and K4 along the edge of the border, PU and K along pillow front edge. Work in St st for 4 rows. BO all sts loosely.

Turn pillow front 90 degrees, PU and K4 along the edge of the border, *PU 2 (from slipped edge sts), M1 using backward loop CO; rep from * to end of slipped edge sts. Work in St st for 4 rows, BO all sts loosely

Turn pillow front 90 degrees, PU and K4 along the edge of the border, PU and K along pillow front edge, PU and K4 along edge of border. Work in St st for 4 rows. BO all sts loosely.

Block piece to 21" square

Pillow Back
CO 108 sts
Row 1: Sl 1, K across.
Row 2: Sl 1, P to last st, K1

Rep Rows 1-2 for 148 rows or 21".

BO all sts. Weave in ends and block to 21" square.

With RS facing, seam 3 sides of the pillow using Mattress St. Turn RS out and insert pillow form. Seam remaining side.

Weave in any remaining ends.

Countless Creative Ideas
TEA FOR TWO!
This book contains 44 charts, featuring mix-and-match designs that celebrate babies & kids, weddings, hobbies, and creative pursuits. Follow the directions for the pillow above to make a throw pillow for the tea and coffee enthusiast in your life, using the following charts: Cup (p. 70), Small Hearts (p.62), Tea Pot (p. 48).

CRAFTY PILLOW

FINISHED MEASUREMENTS
To fit 20" x 20 pillow form, finished size 21" x 21"

YARN
Knit Picks Wool of the Andes (100% Peruvian Highland Wool; 110 yards/50g): MC Indigo Heather 25069, 7 skeins; C1 Haze Heather 26158, 1 skein

NEEDLES
US 7 (4.5mm) straight or circular needles, or size to obtain gauge
US 7 (4.5mm) 40-48" circular needles for border

NOTIONS
Yarn Needle
Stitch Markers
20" Pillow Form

GAUGE
20 sts and 28 rows = 4" in St st, blocked

Crafty Pillow

Notes: Photographed example features the following charts: Spinning Wheel (p. 53), Knitting (p. 51), Crochet (p. 50), Sewing Machine (p. 52). While the charts appears to be rectangular, at gauge they will knit up as a square.

DIRECTIONS
Pillow Front

Choose 4 squares from the charts. Each one is knit the same way, adding the colors via intarsia or duplicate stitch. There is a slipped stitch on each end of the square, which will make it easier to pick up stitches for the border. There are instructions for a plain pillow backing; you can also choose to knit 4 additional squares for decorative back.

Squares
Loosely CO 52 sts.
Row 1: Sl 1, K row 1 of chart to last st, K1
Row 2: Sl 1, P row 2 of chart to last st, K1

Continue in this manner throughout the square. After completing row 70, BO all stitches loosely.

Rep for all squares. If you prefer a solid square, simply follow the same instructions, omitting the chart.

Finishing
Weave in ends. Block each square to 10" x 10".

Arrange the squares in suggested layout or in 2 squares wide x 2 squares long personal layout. With RS facing and using Mattress st, seam the squares together, using MC or preferred color.

Border
With MC, you will knit a small border around the pillow. This will ensure a good fit around your pillow form.

With RS facing and starting with along the right side of the square, *PU 2 (from slipped edge sts), M1 using backward loop CO; rep from * to end of slipped edge sts. Work in St st for 4 rows, BO all sts loosely.

Turn pillow front 90 degrees, PU and K4 along the edge of the border, PU and K along pillow front edge. Work in St st for 4 rows. BO all sts loosely.

Turn pillow front 90 degrees, PU and K4 along the edge of the border, *PU 2 (from slipped edge sts), M1 using backward loop CO; rep from * to end of slipped edge sts. Work in St st for 4 rows, BO all sts loosely

Turn pillow front 90 degrees, PU and K4 along the edge of the border, PU and K along pillow front edge, PU and K4 along edge of border. Work in St st for 4 rows. BO all sts loosely.

Weave in all ends and block piece to 21" square.

Pillow Back
CO 108 sts
Row 1: Sl 1, K across.
Row 2: Sl 1, P to last st, K1

Rep Rows 1-2 for 148 rows or 21".

BO all sts.

Weave in ends and block to 21" square.

With RS facing, seam 3 sides of the pillow using Mattress St. Turn RS out and insert pillow form. Seam remaining side.

Weave in any remaining ends.

Another Idea
GARDEN PARTY

This book contains 44 charts, featuring mix-and-match designs that celebrate babies & kids, weddings, hobbies, and creative pursuits. Follow the directions for the pillow above to make a thoughtful gift for a special gardener, using the following charts: Flowers (p. 72), Watering Can (p.74), Tea Pot (p. 48).

WEDDING AFGHAN

FINISHED MEASUREMENTS
54" square

YARN
Knit Picks Wool of the Andes (100% Peruvian Highland Wool; 110 yards/50g): MC White 24065, 8 skeins, C1 Fjord Heather 25647, 8 skeins, C2 Dove Heather 24077, 6 skeins

NEEDLES
US 7 (4.5mm) straight or circular needles, or size to obtain gauge
US 7 (4.5mm) 40-48" circular needles for border

NOTIONS
Yarn Needle
Stitch Markers

GAUGE
20 sts and 28 rows = 4" in st st, blocked

Wedding Afghan

Notes: Photographed example features the following charts: Wedding Cake (p. 58), Small Hearts (p. 62), Wedding Rings (p. 61), Wedding Bells (p. 64), Heart (p. 63), Entwined Hearts (p. 60), Champagne Glasses (p. 59), Small Alphabet (p. 65). While the charts appears to be rectangular, at gauge they will knit up as a square.

DIRECTIONS

Choose 25 squares from the charts. Each one is knit the same way, adding the colors via intarsia or duplicate stitch. There is a slipped stitch on each end of the square, which will make it easier to seam the squares at the end.

Squares
Loosely CO 52 sts with first color of chart.
Row 1: Sl 1, K row 1 of chart to last st, K1
Row 2: Sl 1, P row 2 of chart to last st, K1

Continue in this manner throughout the square. After completing row 70, BO all stitches loosely.

Rep for all squares. If you prefer a solid square, simply follow the same instructions, omitting the chart.

Finishing

Weave in ends. Block each square to 10" x 10".

Arrange the squares in suggested layout or in 5 squares wide x 5 squares long custom layout. With RS facing and using Mattress st, seam the squares together, using MC or preferred color.

Border
With C2, you will knit a garter st border around the blanket.

Along any side of the afghan, with RS facing PU and knit sts along the edge, being sure to PU 2 sts where squares are joined. Work in garter stitch for 2", BO all sts loosely.

Turn blanket 90 degrees, PU and knit along the edge of the border, PU and knit along blanket edge. Work in garter st for 2". BO all sts loosely.

Turn blanket 90 degrees, PU and knit along the edge of the border, PU and knit along blanket edge. Work in garter st for 2". BO all sts loosely.

Turn blanket 90 degrees, PU and knit along the edge of the border, PU and knit along blanket edge, PU and knit along other edge of border. Work in garter st for 2". BO all sts loosely.

Weave in remaining ends.

Charts

These charts are in grayscale so you can choose your own colors. Although charts appear rectangular, at gauge your finished knit design will be square. Designs can be worked in intarsia or duplicate stitch.

Abbreviations

BO	bind off	P-wise	purlwise
CC	contrast color	rep	repeat
CO	cast on	RH	right hand
cont	continue	rnd(s)	round(s)
dec	decrease(es)	RS	right side
inc	increase	Sk	skip
K	knit	SL	slip
K2tog	knit two sts together	SM	slip marker
K-wise	knitwise	SSK	sl, sl, k these 2 sts tog
LH	left hand	SSP	sl, sl, p these 2 sts tog tbl
M	marker	St st	stockinette stitch
M1	make one stitch	sts	stitch(es)
MC	main color	tog	together
P	purl	WE	work even
P2tog	purl 2 sts together	WS	wrong side
PM	place marker	WYIB	with yarn in back
PU	pick up	WYIF	with yarn in front

Legend

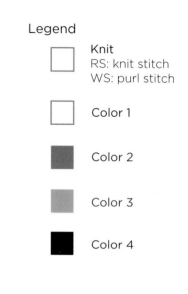

Knit
RS: knit stitch
WS: purl stitch

Color 1

Color 2

Color 3

Color 4

Football Chart

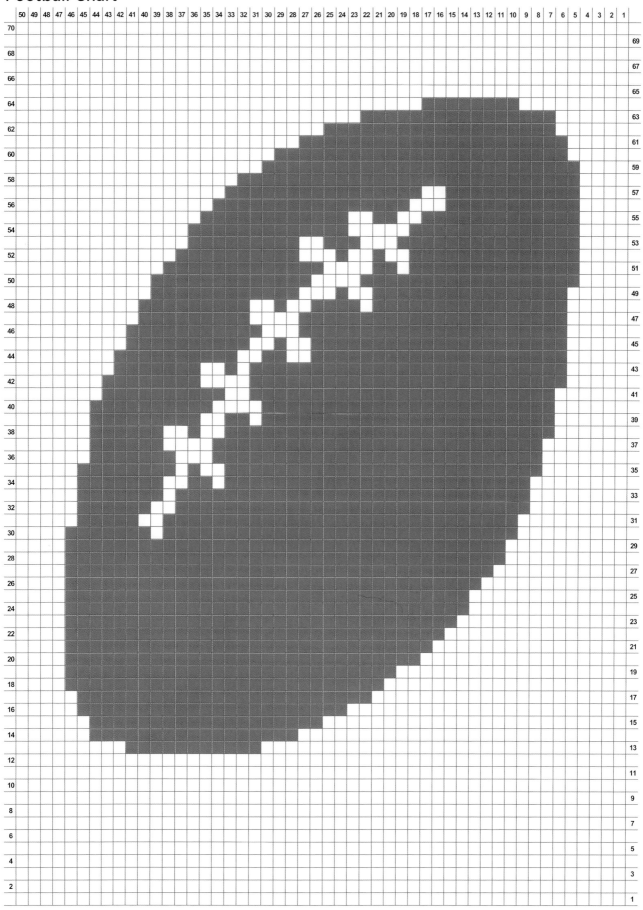

Horizontal Stripes Chart

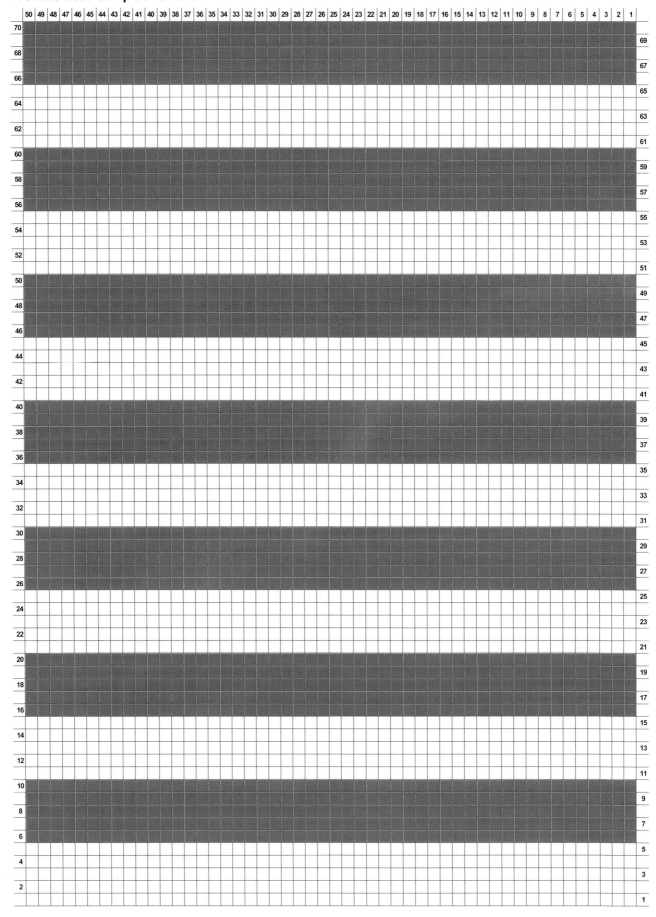

Stars Chart

Vertical Stripes Chart

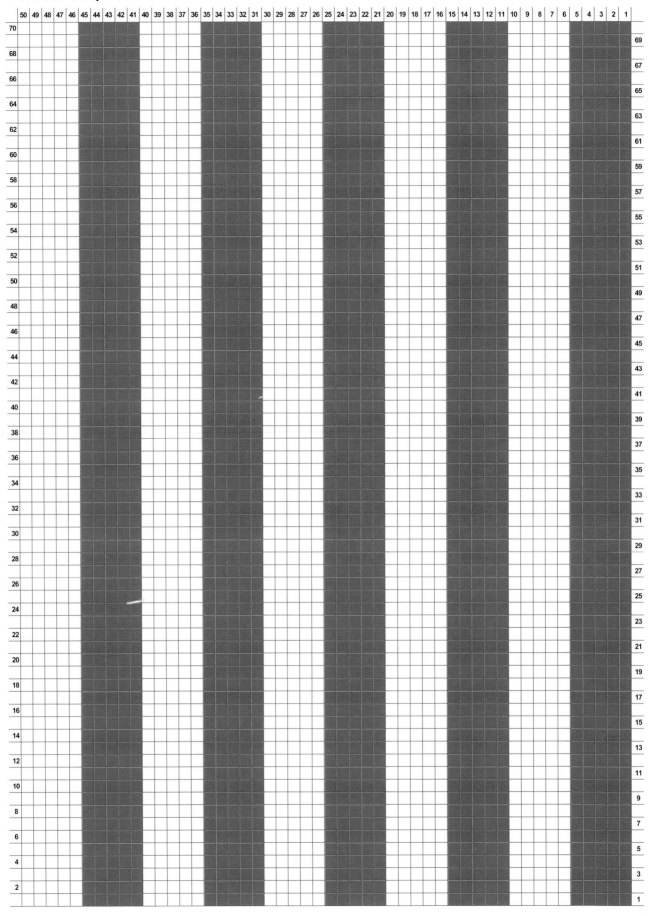

Baby Blocks Chart

Balloons Chart

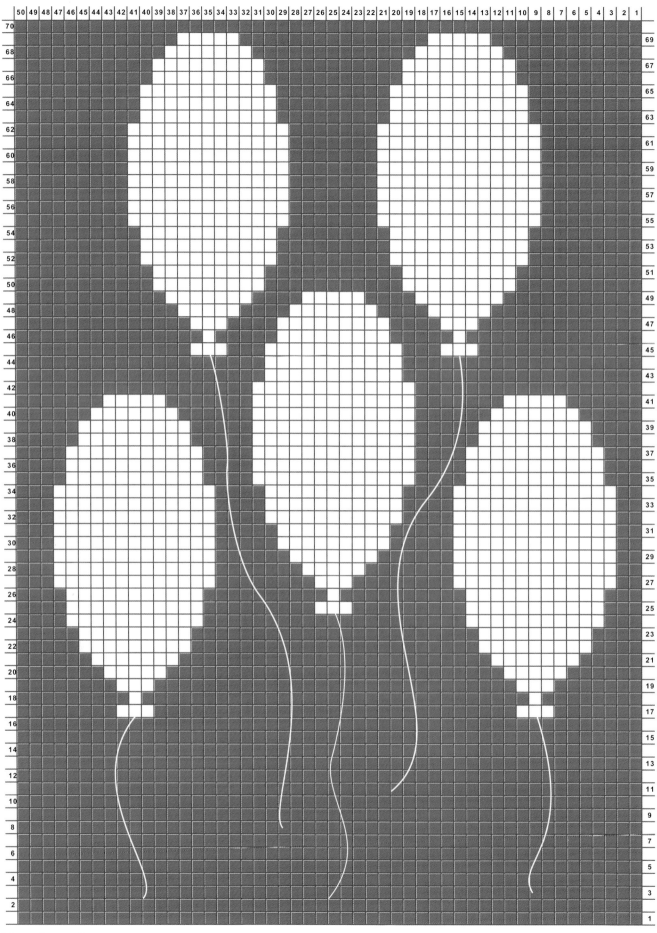

Teddy Bear Chart

Bunny Chart

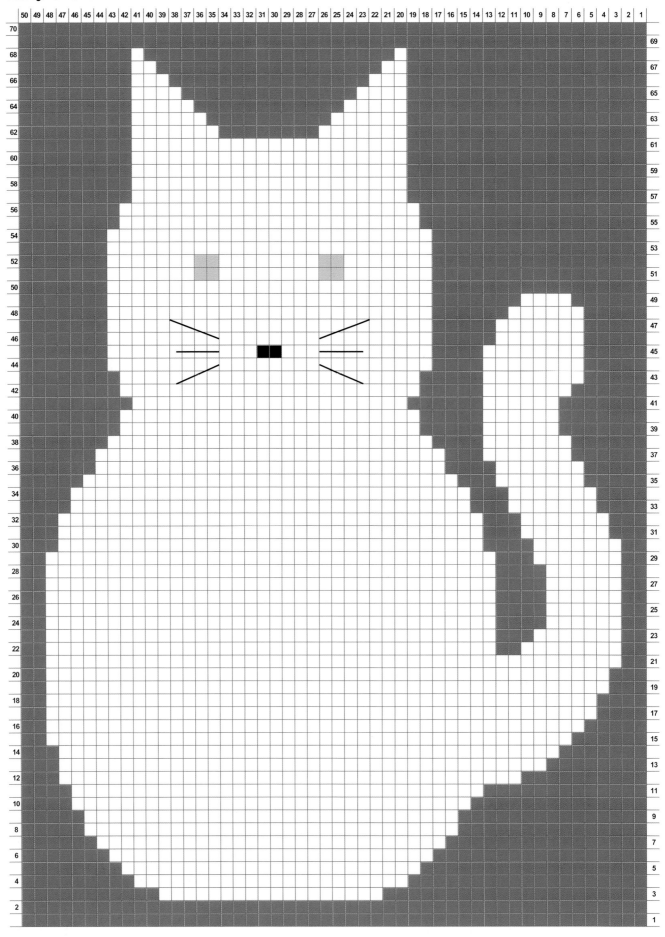

Owl Chart

Rattle Chart

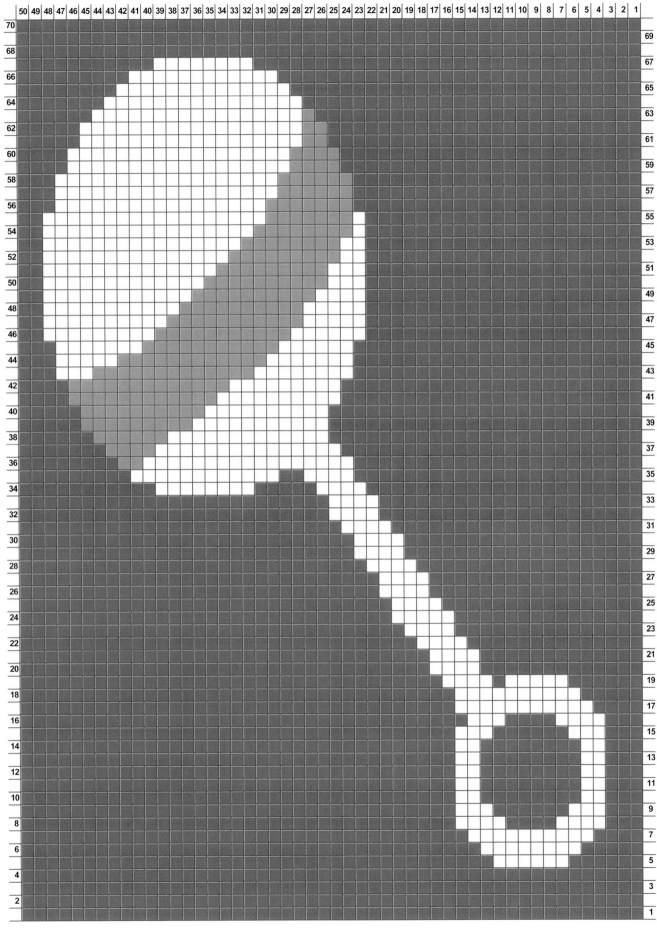

Star Chart

Stork Chart

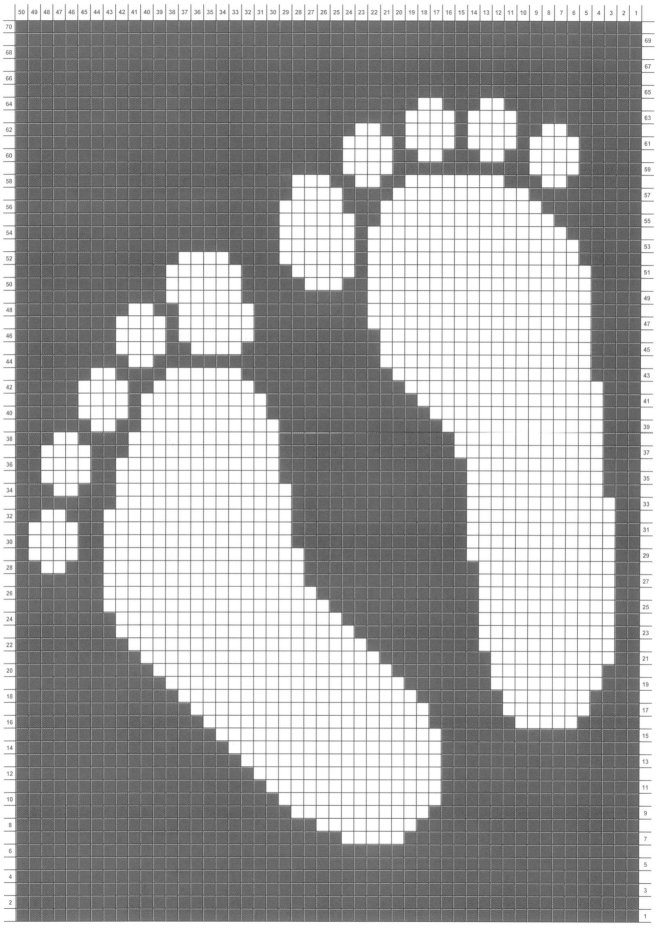

Mixer Chart

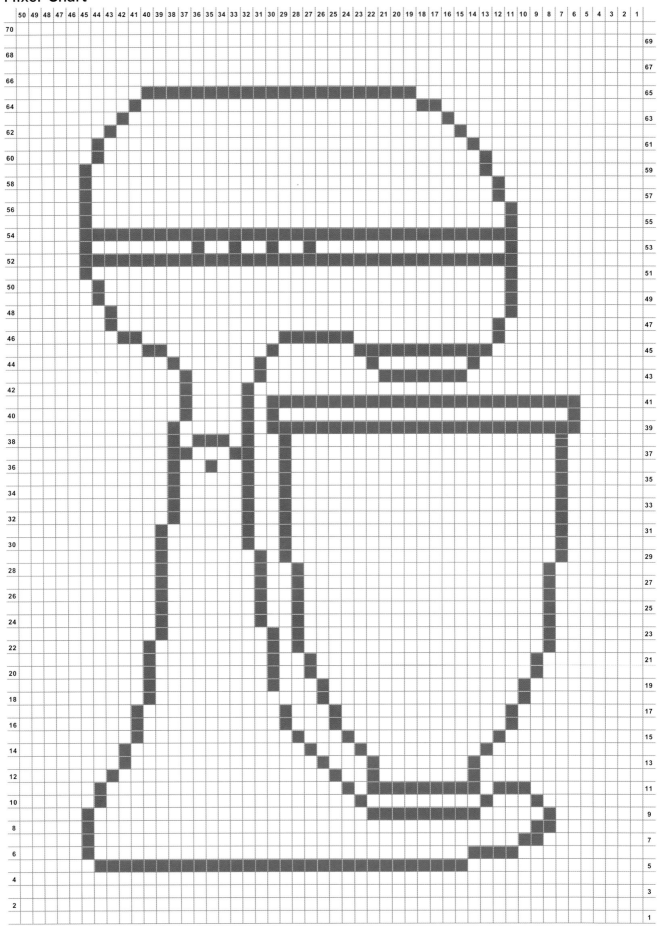

Pie Chart

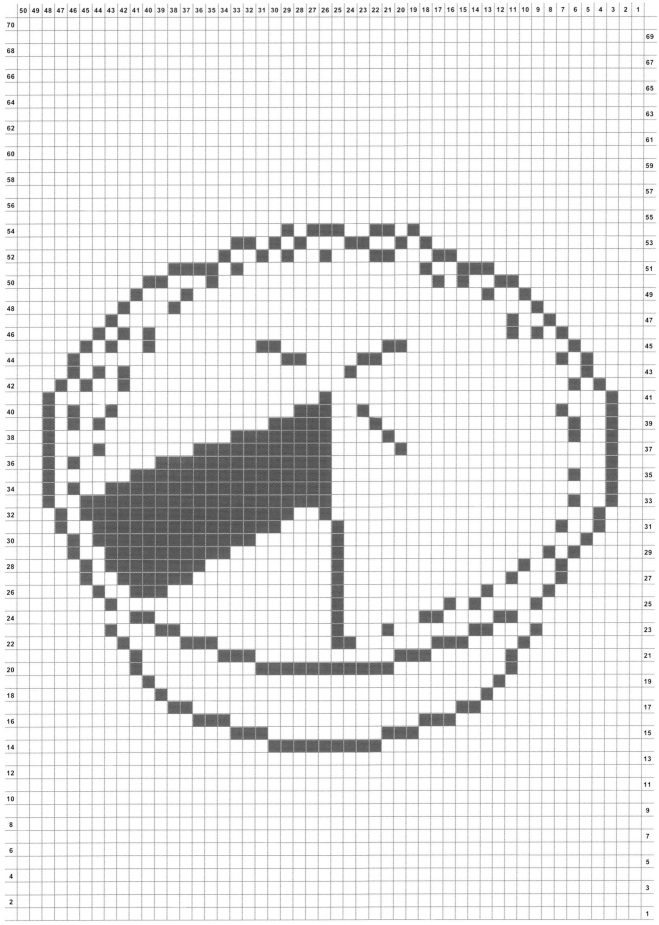

Teapot Chart

Whisk and Spoon Chart

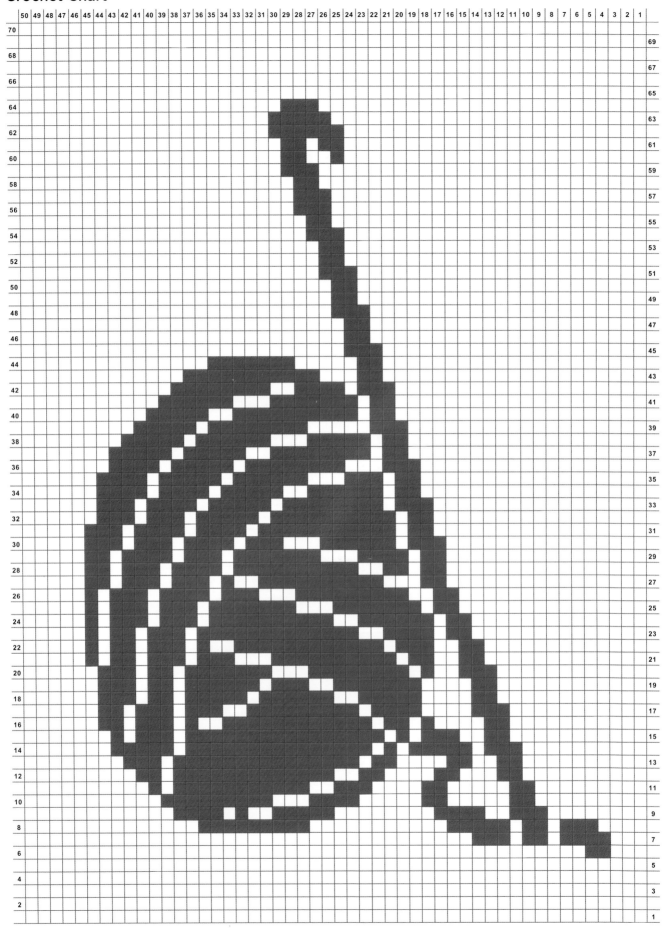

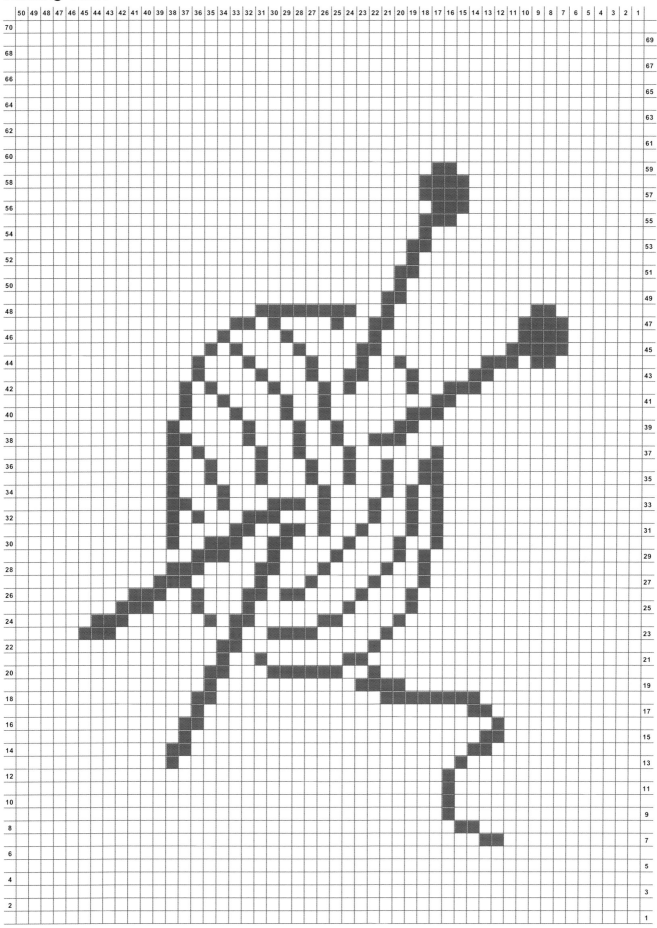

Sewing Machine Chart

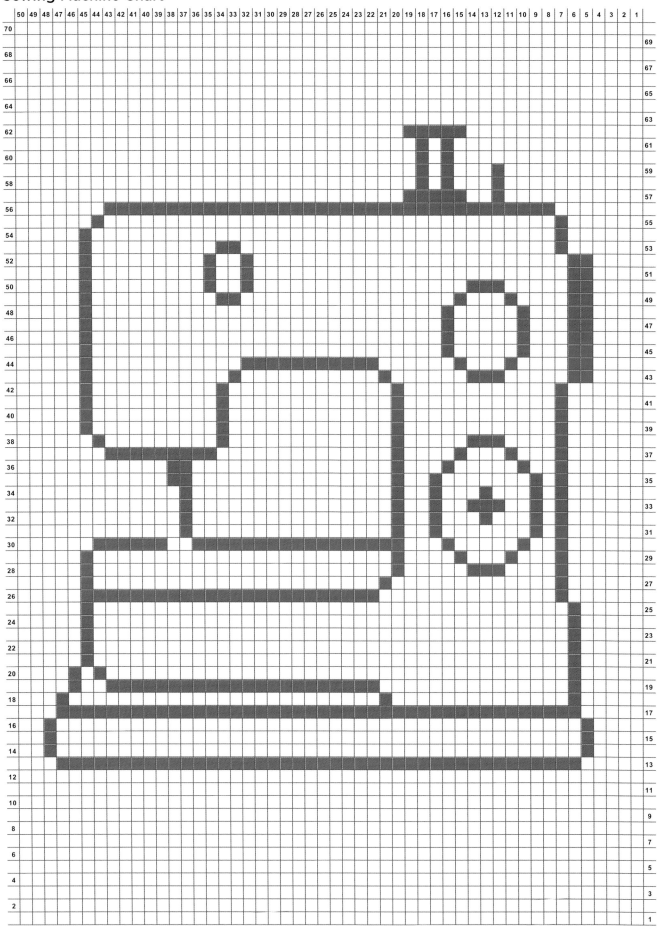

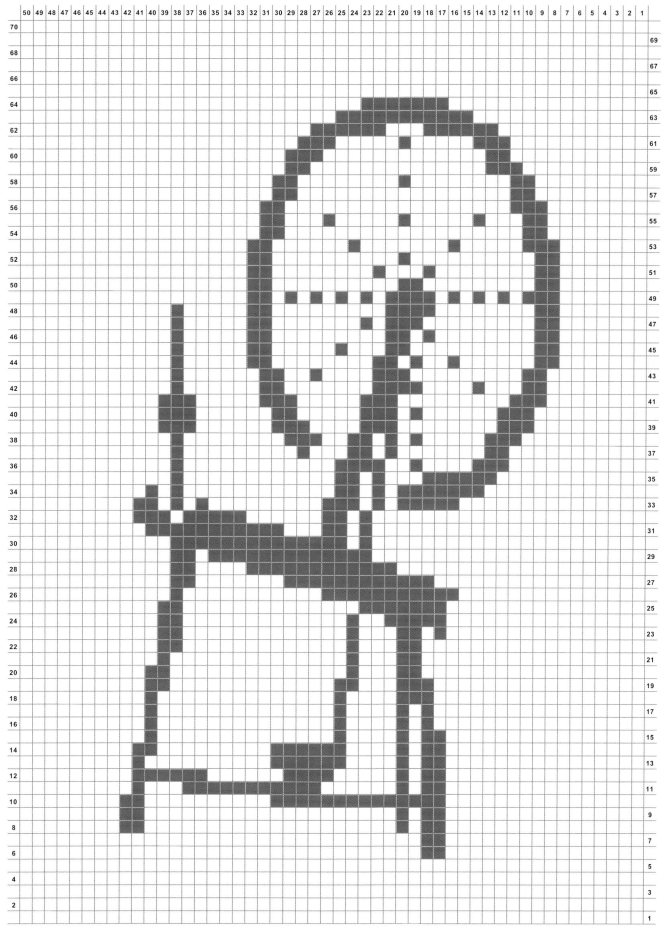

Bike Chart

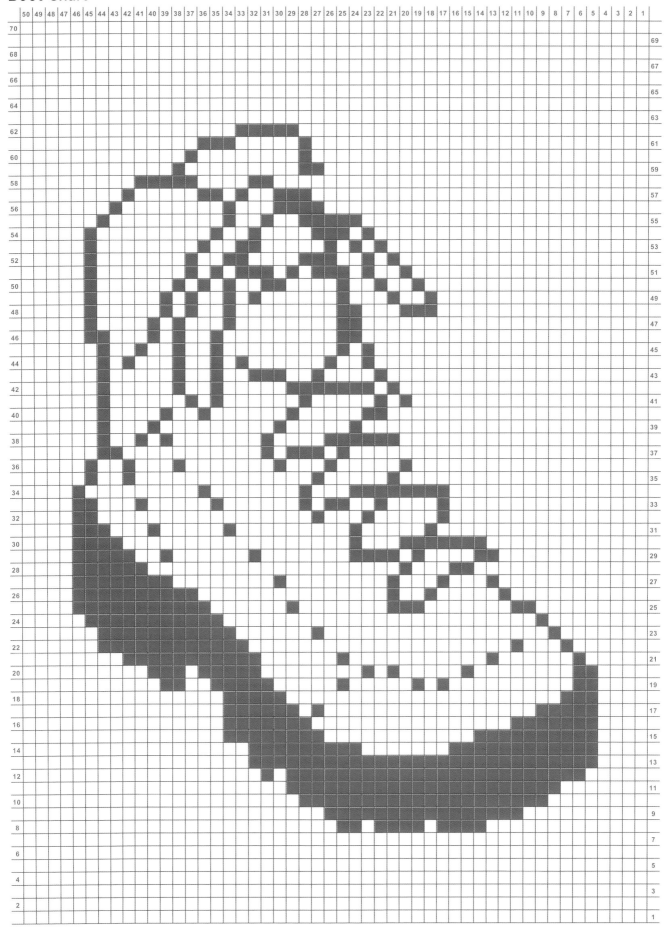

RV Chart

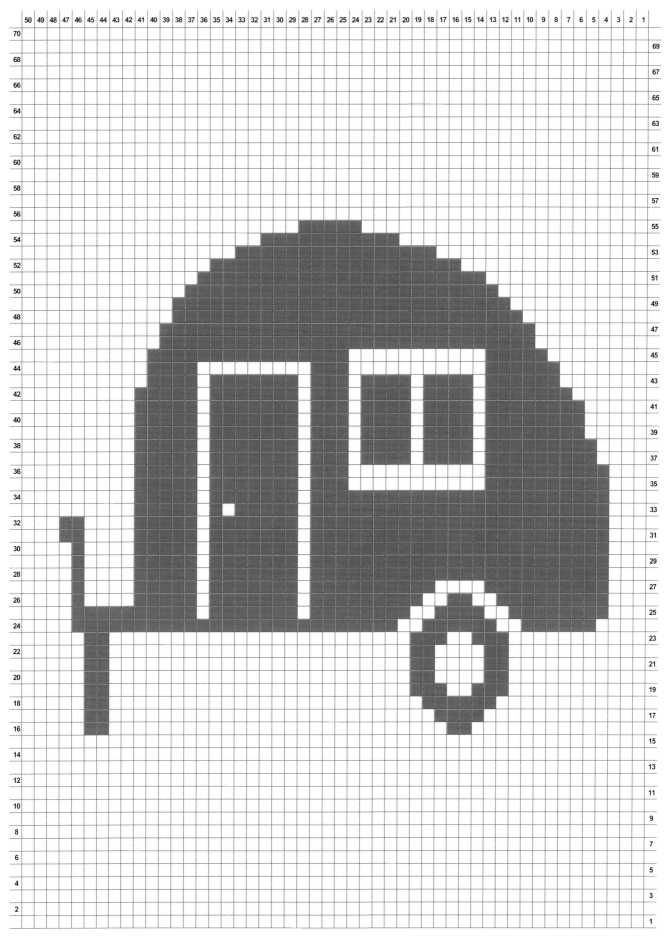

Wedding Cake Chart

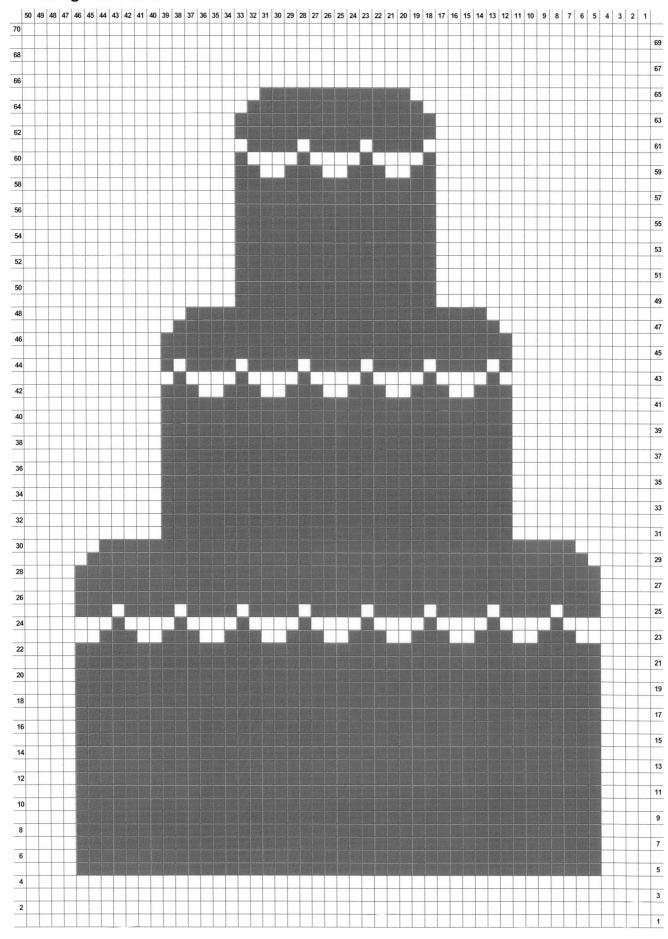

Champagne Glasses Charts

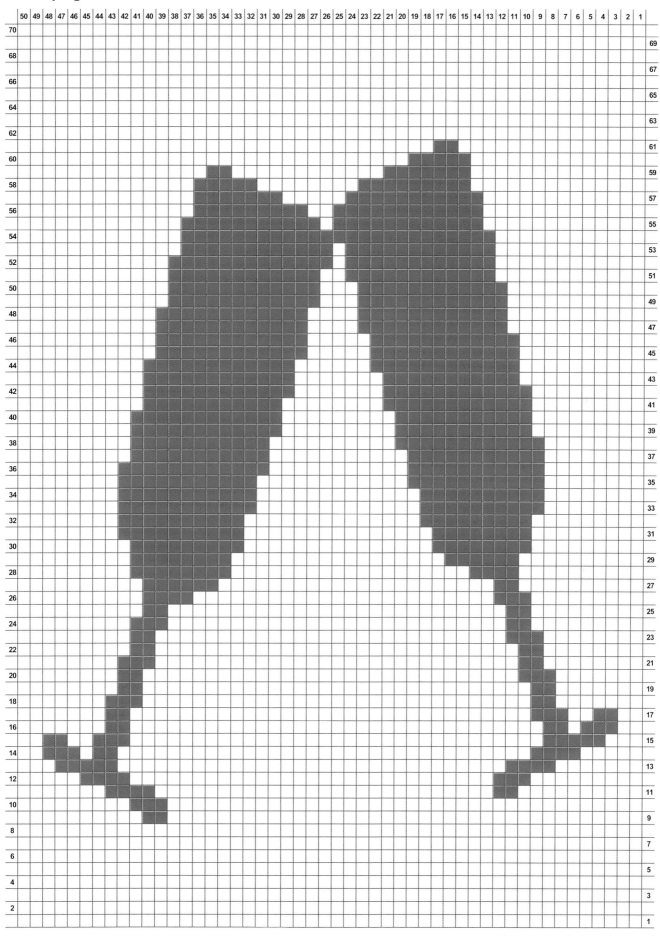

Wedding Rings Chart

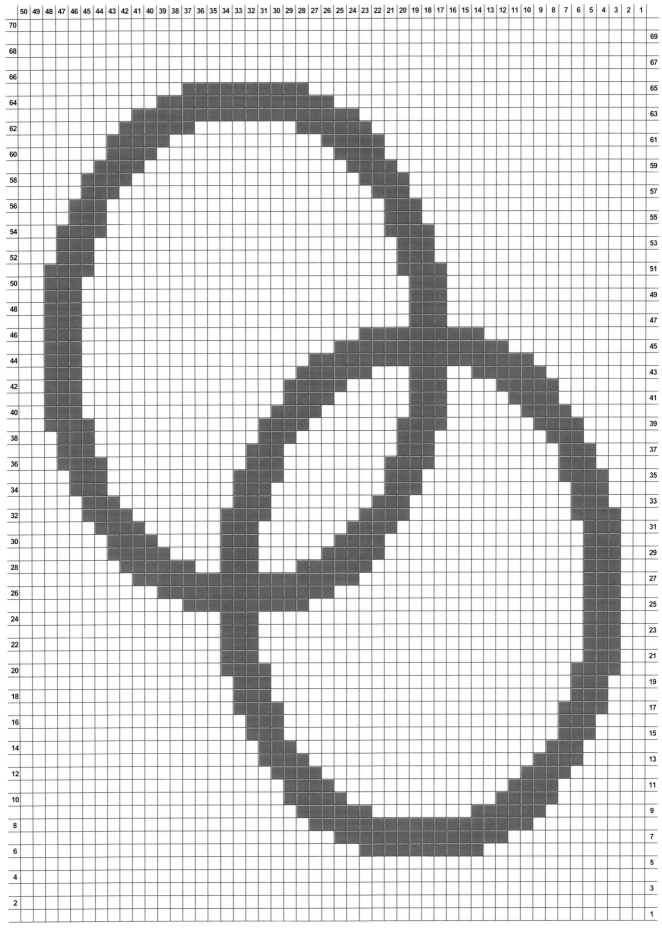

Small Hearts Chart

Heart Chart

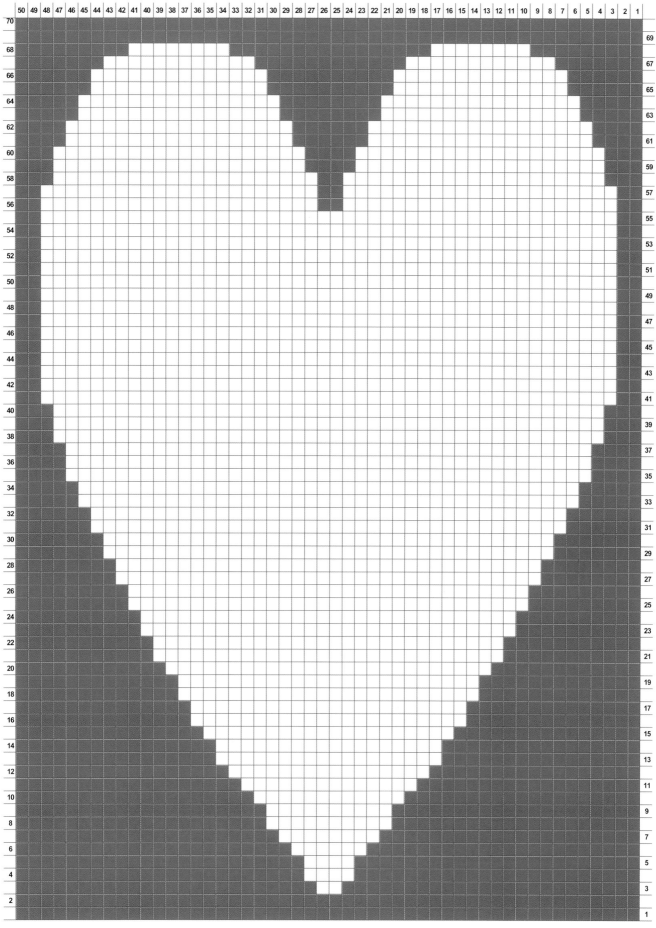

Small Alphabet Chart

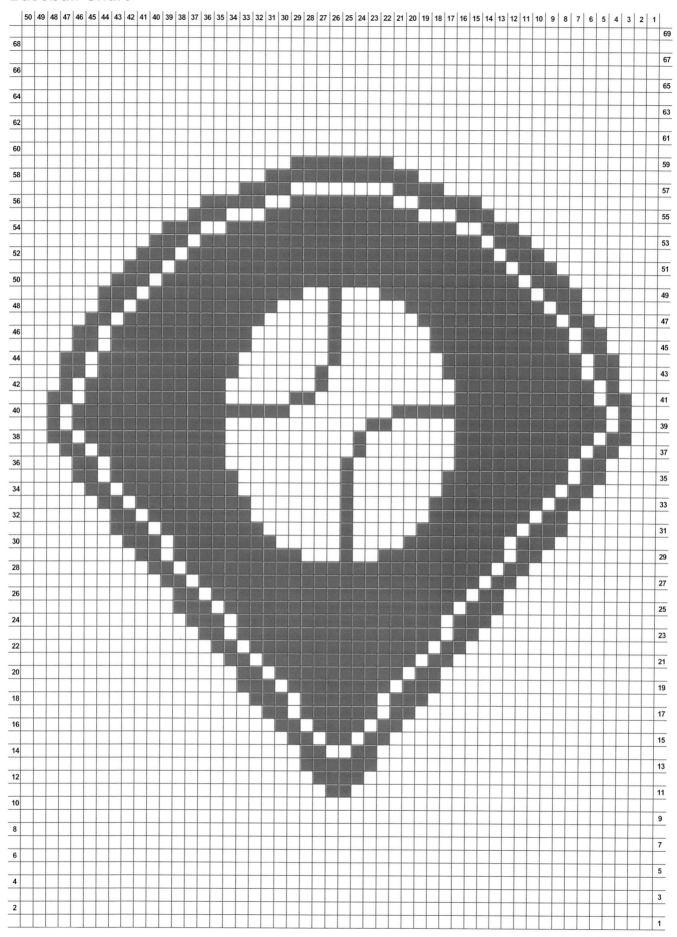

Sailboat Chart

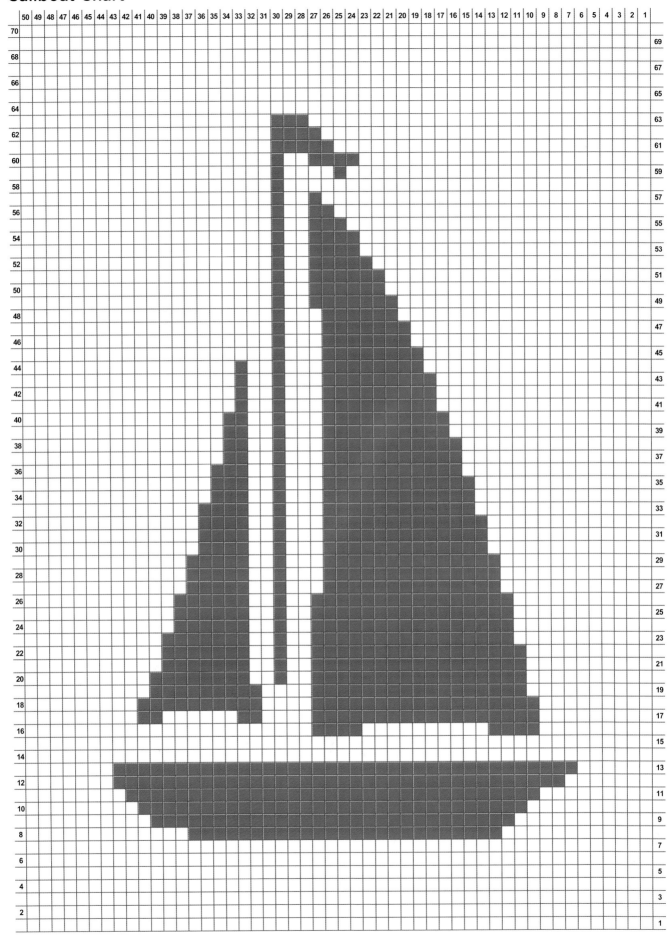

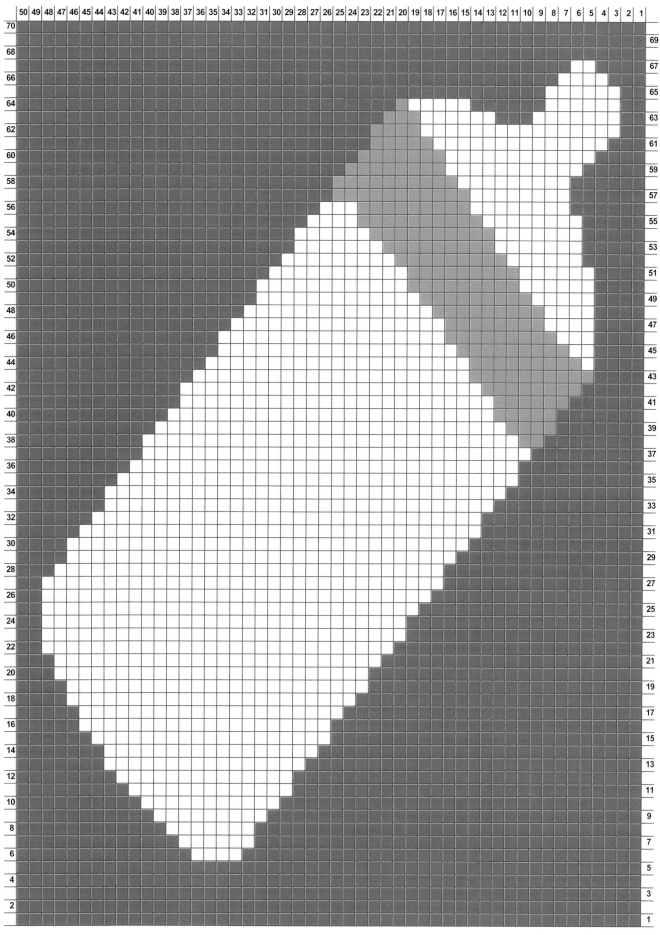

Cup Chart

Double Heart Chart

Flowers Chart

Soccer Chart

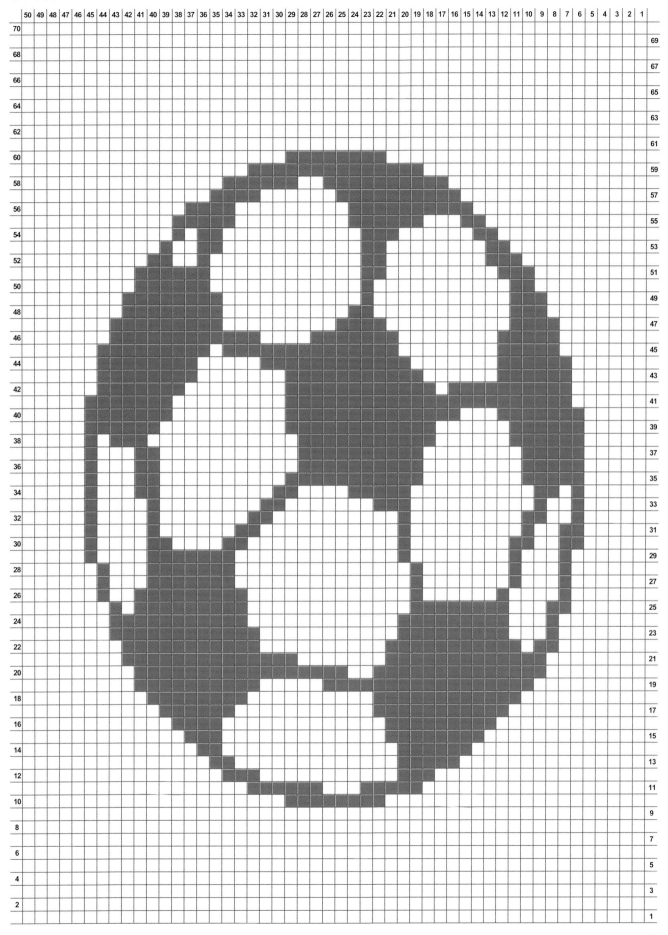

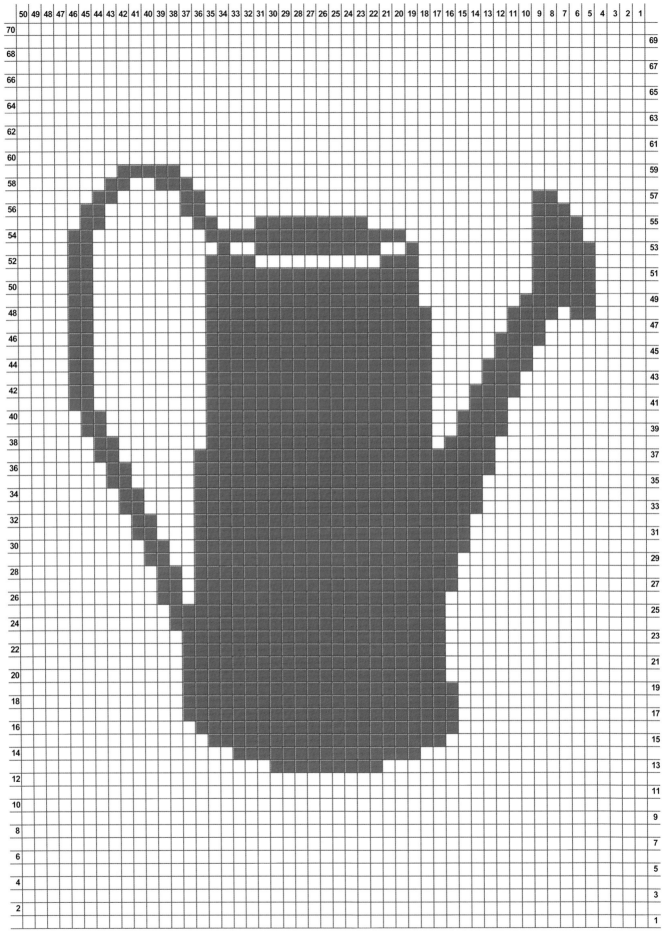

Blank Chart - capture more memories with your own design!

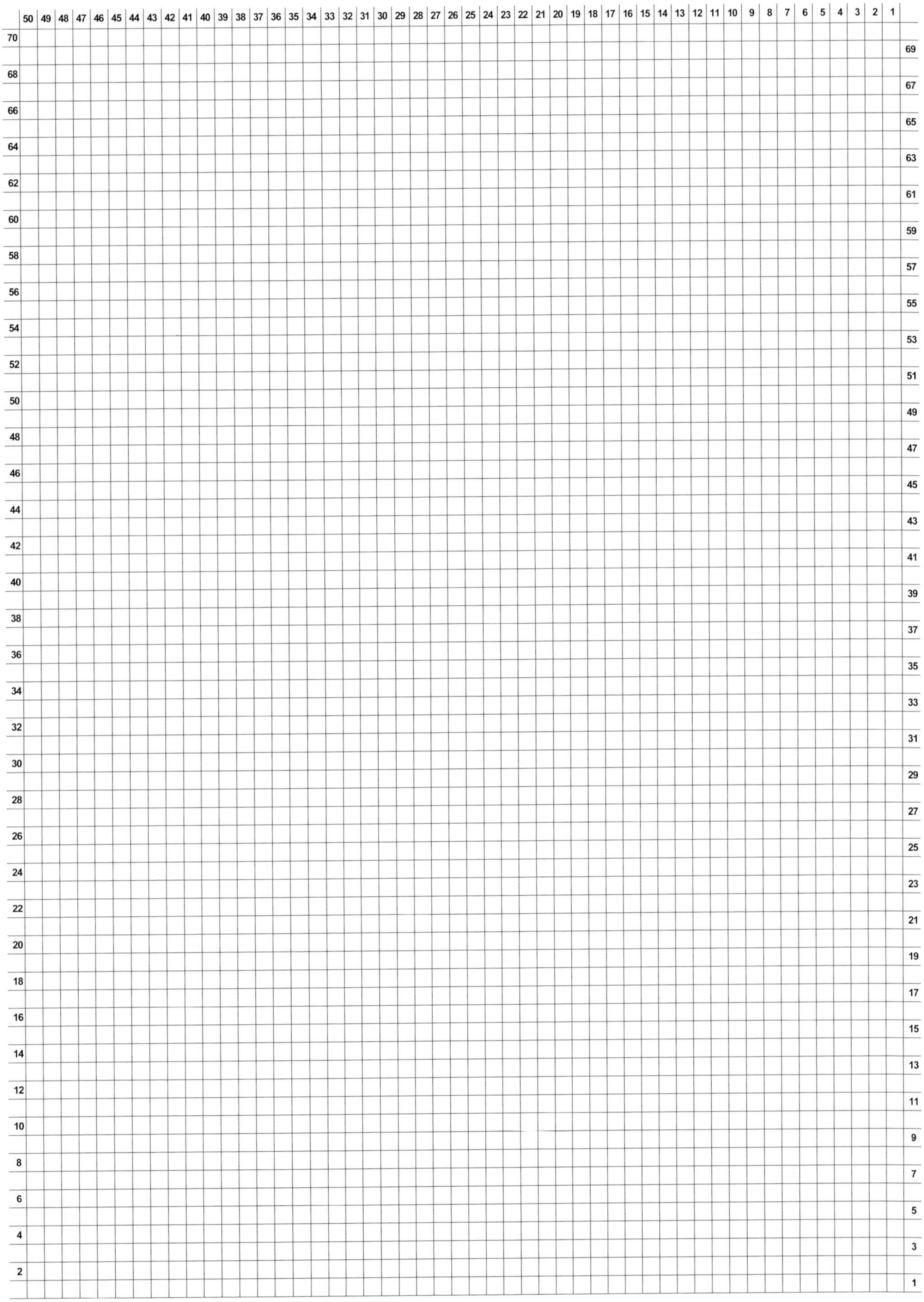

Knit Picks®

Knit Picks yarn is both luxe and affordable—a seeming contradiction trounced! But it's not just about the pretty colors; we also care deeply about fiber quality and fair labor practices, leaving you with a gorgeously reliable product you'll turn to time and time again.

THIS COLLECTION FEATURES

Wool of the Andes
Worsted Weight
100% Peruvian Highland Wool

View these beautiful yarns and more at www.KnitPicks.com